Viola Time Runners

Piano accompaniment book

Kathy and David Blackwell

T0057029

Teacher's note

These piano parts are written to accompany the tunes in *Viola Time Runners*. They are an alternative to the viola duet accompaniments or audio tracks, and are not designed to be used with those items. A separate violin piano accompaniment book is available providing parts for when violas play together with violins using *Fiddle Time Runners*.

Kathy and David Blackwell

OXFORD
UNIVERSITY PRESS

OXFORD
UNIVERSITY PRESS
Great Clarendon Street, Oxford OX2 6DP,
United Kingdom

Oxford University Press is a department of the University of Oxford.
It furthers the University's objective of excellence in research, scholarship,
and education by publishing worldwide. Oxford is a registered trade mark of
Oxford University Press in the UK and in certain other countries

This collection Oxford University Press 2005, 2013, and 2023.

Unless marked otherwise, all pieces are by Kathy and David Blackwell and are
© Oxford University Press. All traditional and composed pieces are
arranged by Kathy and David Blackwell and are © Oxford University Press.
Unauthorized arrangement or photocopying of this copyright material is ILLEGAL

Kathy and David Blackwell have asserted their right under the Copyright,
Designs and Patents Act, 1988, to be identified as the Composers of this Work

Database right Oxford University Press (maker)

Impression: 1

All rights reserved. No part of this publication may be reproduced,
stored in a retrieval system, or transmitted, in any form or by any means,
without the prior permission in writing of Oxford University Press

Permission to perform the works in this anthology in public
(except in the course of divine worship) should normally be obtained from
a local performing right licensing organization, unless the owner or the occupier
of the premises being used already holds a licence from such an organization.
Likewise, permission to make and exploit a recording of these works
should be obtained from a local mechanical copyright licensing organization

Enquiries concerning reproduction outside the scope of the above
should be directed to the Music Rights Department, Oxford University Press, at
music.permissions.uk@oup.com or at the address above

ISBN 978-019-336620-0

Cover illustration by Martin Remphry

Music and text origination Katie Johnston and Julia Bovee
Printed in Great Britain

Contents

1. Start the show 4
2. Banyan tree (*duet*) 6
3. Heat haze 7
4. Medieval tale 8
5. In memory 9
6. Chase in the dark 10
7. Merrily danced the Quaker's wife 11
8. O leave your sheep (*duet*) 14
9. Jingle bells (J. Pierpont) 12
10. Allegretto in C (Mozart) 15
11. The Mallow fling 16
12. Noël (Daquin) (*duet*) 17
13. Finale from the 'Water Music' (Handel) 18
14. Ecossaise in G (Beethoven) 19
15. Viola Time rag 20
16. Busy day (*duet*) 22
17. On the go! 23
18. Blue whale 26
18. Yodelling song (*alternative*) 47
19. Takin' it easy 24
20. Mean street chase 27
20. Romani band (*alternative*) 48
21. Ten thousand miles away (*duet*) 28
22. I got those viola blues 30
23. Air in C (J. C. Bach) 32
24. Prelude from 'Te Deum' (Charpentier) 33
25. That's how it goes! 34
26. Flamenco dance 36
27. Somebody's knocking at your door 38
28. The old chariot 39
29. Adam in the garden 40
30. Air (Handel) (*duet*) 44
31. The wee cooper o' Fife 42
32. Aerobics! 45
33. Caribbean sunshine 46

1. Start the show

KB & DB

13
f
f
17
mf cresc.
mf cresc.
f
f
21
mf
mf
25
f
f

2. Banyan tree

C string special

Jamaican folk tune

3. Heat haze

KB & DB

4. Medieval tale

KB & DB

5. In memory

for Eileen

C string special

KB & DB

6. Chase in the dark

KB & DB

7. Merrily danced the Quaker's wife

Scottish folk tune

8. O leave your sheep: page 14

9. Jingle bells

J. Pierpont

Nos. 8 and 9 are reversed to avoid a page turn.

17
mf
mf
21
25
29
cresc.
cresc.
D.C. al Fine

8. O leave your sheep

C string special

French folk tune

10. Allegretto in C

Mozart

11. The Mallow fling

Irish folk tune

12. Noël

C string special

Daquin

13. Finale from the 'Water Music'

Handel

14. Ecossaise in G

Beethoven

15. Viola Time rag

KB & DB

17
f
mp
f
mp
22
27
mf
mf
32
cresc.
f
cresc.
f
8vb

16. Busy day

17. On the go!

KB & DB

* The repeat is written out in full in the viola part.

18. *Blue whale:* page 26

19. Takin' it easy

KB & DB

* The repeat is written out in full in the viola part.
Nos. 18 and 19 are reversed to avoid a page turn.

17
21
mf
25
cresc.
cresc.
poco rit.
CODA
41
pizz.
p
p

18. Blue whale

C string special

KB & DB

20. Mean street chase

C string special

KB & DB

21. Ten thousand miles away

C string special

Sea shanty

13
Fine
cresc.
cresc.
(16)
mp
mf
mp
mf
21
f
f
25
D.C. al Fine

22. I got those viola blues

KB & DB

13
f
mf
f
16
f
mf
mf
f
20
f
mf
f
24
rall.
mp
f
mf
mp
f

23. Air in C

24. Prelude from 'Te Deum'

Charpentier

25. That's how it goes!

KB & DB

13
16
mp
mp
19
cresc.
cresc.
22
D.C. al Fine
f
f

26. Flamenco dance

KB & DB

25
mp
4
mp
32
pizz.
f
f
39
arco
f
4
f
46
cresc.
ff
marcato cresc.
ff

27. Somebody's knocking at your door

Spiritual

28. The old chariot

Sea shanty

29. Adam in the garden

Jamaican folk tune

21
f
f
27
f
f
33
mp
mp
39
f
f

30. *Air:* page 44

31. The wee cooper o' Fife

Scottish folk tune

Nos. 30 and 31 are reversed to avoid a page turn.

13
mf
mp
16
20
cresc.
cresc.
mf
24
Slower
mp
p

30. Air

Handel

32. Aerobics!

KB & DB

33. Caribbean sunshine

KB & DB

18. Yodelling song

German folk tune

This piece is an alternative to No. 18 Blue whale (C string special) and can be found in the Ensemble parts section of the pupil book.

20. Romani band

KB & DB

This piece is an alternative to No. 20 Mean street chase (C string special) and can be found in the Ensemble parts section of the pupil book.